MOUNT MARY COLLEGE LIBRARY
Milwaukee, Wisconsin 53222

WITHDRAWN

D0856542

The Patrick and Beatrice Haggerty
Library
Mount Mary College

Presented by

MARY POTTER

THE PARKS
SQUARES & MEWS OF
LONDON

MOUNT MARY COLLEGE LIBRARY
Milwaukee, Wisconsin 53222

THE PARKS SQUARES & MEWS OF LONDON

Principal photography
NICOLAI CANETTI

Commentary
SANDY LESBERG

82- 121

PEEBLES PRESS
New York   London

FIRST PUBLISHED 1976 BY
PEEBLES PRESS INTERNATIONAL
12 Thayer St., London W1M 5LD
10 Columbus Circle, New York, N.Y. 10019

Designed by Nicolai Canetti

© Peebles Press International (Europe) Ltd
ISBN 0–672–52222–5
Library of Congress Catalog No. 75–36328

All rights reserved. No part of this book may be reproduced in
any form or by any means, except for the inclusion
of brief quotations in a review, without permission in writing from the publisher.

The publishers wish to acknowledge with great gratitude the splendid assistance
and co-operation they have received in the preparation of this book
from the British Tourist Authority

Distributed by
The Bobbs-Merrill Co. Inc.
4300 West 62nd St., Indianapolis, Indiana 46268, U.S.A
in the United States and Canada

WHS Distributors
Euston St., Freemen's Common, Leicester, England
in the U.K., Ireland, Australia, New Zealand and South Africa

Meulenhoff-Bruna B.V.
Beulingstraat 2, Amsterdam, Netherlands
in the Netherlands

Printed and bound in the U.K. by
Redwood Burn Limited, Trowbridge and Esher

914.21
L56

Will there always be an England? Perhaps not, but while she's here we should all take notice of her good, essential sturdiness that demonstrates the potential for survival of any people determined to last through quite a few very trying centuries. To many, England means London and London stands for dignity, continuity, rich tradition, clarity of right-thinking and an unshakeable commitment to clearly defined purposes. She has been quietly and steadfastly defying the mad rush of most of the rest of the world into shrieking disarray and discomfort. Here, in London, is where yesterday, today and tomorrow can meet in unsettled fragile congress under a flag of truce albeit well clouded by torrents of mutual mistrust.

For a traditionalist London is the most necessary place that ever was conceived. For those more inclined toward looking around unknown corners and over unfamiliar mountain tops there is a certain comfort to be gained in the realization that the old place is fundamentally the same as she's always been.

London began as a collection of small neighbouring villages that gradually intertwined until the large municipal body we know today was ultimately formed. But each of these smaller communities maintained its own village green, its own breathing area, its own special open space that was never allowed to be smothered by the exingencies of a growing society. And that is the way London is today, a large, sprawling, commercial and industrial metropolis that is graced by hundreds of parks and squares that provide the unique green open spaces so required by all Londoners. This is the great delight of the city, that you may wander down a busy shopping street, choc-a-block full of people, turn a corner and be in a completely isolated area of peace and tranquility and only one hundred good steps separate one from the other. Some people have falsely assumed that England is a nation of shopkeepers, but that is not the case at all. England is rather a nation of gardeners, and London, for all its being crowded with people and shops, hotels and the other accoutrements of a modern capital city, has managed to provide all manner of internal spaces to accommodate the performance of carefully tended grassy lawns and coloured flower beds that contribute so importantly to satisfying that need for greenery.

The history of London has been, since the time of Charles I, one of evolution rather than revolution. England is the most active monarchy in the world yet the country is one of the most heavily industrialised, and to a great extent, one of the most socialized in all the world. Here, the trappings of royalty are readily available to anyone. You can rent a Rolls Royce from Avis for just the day if you like, or moor your hired yacht in St. Katharine's Yacht Basin while lunching at the Tower Hotel in the shadow of the Tower of London – a more pleasant manner of visiting the Tower than some real royalty have done in years gone by.

At the other end of the spectrum, Londoners can be treated medically for little or no cost and would never be faced with genuine destitution or starvation.

It is a remarkable accommodation of contemporary societal interests, and is more viable and successful, given all its drawbacks and problems, than most other systems.

Here is where the traditional and the modern live side by side, one complementing the other with graceful ease. An old London coach house becomes a charming modern mews house, a once single-familied Victorian mansion has been converted into modern flats, but there is always the undiluted pleasure of being able to see, amidst the obviously successful transition to a modern civilised city, so much of God's good green earth in so many delightful patches scattered all over this city of London.

Hyde Park along the Serpentine.

Sailing in the middle of London, on the Serpentine.

Speakers Corner, Hyde Park, where anyone can have his say.

Some speakers exude personality . . .

. . . Some are more subdued.

Hyde Park also provides sleeping quarters.

An outdoor concert at Kenwood Park.

A swan in the middle of some ducks in St. James's Park.

Feeding time at St. James's Park.

MOUNT MARY COLLEGE LIBRARY
Milwaukee, Wisconsin 53222

Riding in Rotten Row, Hyde Park.

82- 121

Parks are for being played in, too.

Modern art along Piccadilly.

The technique of feeding pigeons —
similar to determining if it is still raining.

Joy among friends.

Queen Victoria continues to survey one of the Royal Parks.

Small reclining figure in the landscape in Regents Park.

Two reclining figures in the landscape in Regents Park — one alert, one asleep.

Scenes in Hyde Park – surrounded by a very busy
London and yet so peaceful and removed.

A formal garden in Holland Park.

I know it's here somewhere.

Kensington Gardens.

The Albert Memorial in Kensington Gardens.

Man and dogs at play beside the Serpentine in Hyde Park.

The view from Holland Park.

Some of the local inhabitants of Richmond Park.

44

Pelicans in St. James's Park.

Hyde Park.

Blooming time.

Sparrows not quite spoonfed.

Open air music.

The Orangery, Kensington Gardens.

Regents Park Canal.

46

Artist in Kensington Gardens.

Cat among the chrysanthemums at Central Park's Glasshouses.

Pelicans at St. James's Park.

hat with a Royal Park's Gatekeeper.

Afloat in Regents Park.

Open air music.

Laburnum Arbor, Hampton Court.

Everyone must rest from time to time.

Grosvenor Square – The Roosevelt Memorial.

You'll always find some greenery, even when there's not room for a full sized park.

Note the old lamp.

This magnificent towering oak graces one of the entrances to Lincoln's Inn Fields.

I'm really just sitting here enjoying the park.

Well, maybe a quick bite.

Many London squares are for the
private use of the local residents.

Regardless of the surroundings there
will always be places for children to play.

One of the fountains in Russell Square.

Albert Memorial.

Holland Park.

Some well fed plants in the tropical
greenhouse at Kew Gardens.

St. James's Park in the sunlight.

Regents Park, in chilly springtime.

Some Canadian visitors join the lunchtime crowds at St. James's Park.

Lifeguards on the move.

One of the several secluded Inns of Court.

. . . Some on them.

Two men contemplating a pigeon,
contemplating two men.

Queens Gate Mews.

Street corner consultation in Belgrave Square.

Any seat will do in Belgrave Square.

A well-greened mews house.

The Royal Borough of Kensington
KYNANCE
MEWS. S.W.7.

A Hampstead mews is quiet and solitary in the rain . . .

. . . while Holland Park Mews bustles with activity.

Cheval Place, South Kensington.

The Water Mews beside the Tower Hotel,
with Tower Bridge in the background.

Each mews entrance has its own view, some old . . .

. . . Some new.

This mews designed for horses, is nearly a century older than

this mews designed for automobiles.

Queens Gate Mews.

Charles Dickens' House, Gough Square.

Lennox Gardens Mews.

cobbled mews street lined with brick houses; a garage door marked 12, parked cars, potted plants, and ivy-covered walls under an overcast sky

Upper Cheyne Walk.

Everything is quite neat at Henniker Mews, even the rubbish bin.

As long as there are different coloured
paints mews houses will never look alike.

A pair of very old mews' entrances.

This will undoubtedly convert to a mews house eventually, but for now it is in its primary usage.

82- 121   914.21
                                           L56

Lesberg, Sandy.
The parks, squares and mews of
London.

Mount Mary College
Library
Milwaukee, Wisconsin 53222